THE 9 LAWS
OF WEALTH

A Comprehensive Guide to Building
Financial Success and Security

Janie Dolan

INTRODUCTION

The Importance of Wealth and Financial Freedom

Wealth and financial freedom are important for various reasons. Financial freedom allows you to live the life you want, without having to worry about money constantly. It gives you the flexibility to choose your career, invest in your future, and pursue your dreams. Having wealth also enables you to have more options in life, such as the ability to travel, buy a house, and retire comfortably.

Moreover, wealth and financial freedom can help reduce stress and increase overall happiness. Financial stress is one of the leading causes of stress and anxiety, and by achieving financial freedom, you can alleviate that stress and live a more fulfilling life.

Additionally, wealth and financial freedom give you the opportunity to help others. By having more resources, you can make a positive impact on your community and contribute to causes that you care about. Overall, wealth and financial freedom are crucial to living a fulfilling life.

The 9 Laws of Wealth

There are various principles and guidelines that can help you achieve wealth and financial freedom. One popular framework is the 9 Laws of Wealth. These laws were developed by self-made millionaire and author, Stuart Wilde. The 9 Laws of Wealth are as follows:

1. **The Law of Purpose:** You must have a clear purpose or goal for your wealth. This means having a vision of what you want to achieve and why it's important to you.

2. **The Law of Self-Discipline:** Wealth requires discipline and focus. You must have the self-discipline to stick to your plan and make sacrifices when necessary.

3. **The Law of Integrity:** Wealth is built on a foundation of honesty and integrity. You must be true to yourself and others in all your financial dealings.

4. **The Law of Persistence:** Wealth requires persistence and resilience. You must be willing to work hard and persevere through challenges and setbacks.

5. **The Law of Association:** You are the sum of the people you surround yourself with. To achieve wealth, you must associate with people who have a positive mindset and support your goals.

6. **The Law of Visualization:** You must visualize your success and believe that it's possible. Visualization helps you stay focused and motivated towards your goals.

7. **The Law of Belief:** Your beliefs and mindset shape your reality. To achieve wealth, you must have a positive mindset and believe that wealth is attainable for you.

8. **The Law of Action:** Wealth requires action. You must take consistent and deliberate action towards your goals.

9. **The Law of Gratitude:** Gratitude attracts more abundance into your life. You must be grateful for what you have and celebrate your successes along the way.

How Following These Laws Can Change Your Financial Future

By following the 9 Laws of Wealth, you can transform your financial future. Here are some ways these laws can benefit you:

1. **Clarity of purpose:** By having a clear purpose for your wealth, you can stay focused and motivated towards your goals. You'll have a greater sense of direction and purpose in your financial decisions.

2. **Self-discipline:** Self-discipline is a key factor in achieving wealth and financial freedom. By developing this skill, you can stay on track towards your goals and make sacrifices when necessary.

3. **Integrity:** Building wealth on a foundation of honesty and integrity helps you build trust and credibility with others. This can lead to more opportunities and better financial outcomes.

4. **Persistence:** Wealth requires persistence and resilience. By persevering through challenges and setbacks, you can develop the skills and mindset needed to achieve your financial goals.

5. **Association:** Surrounding yourself with positive and supportive people can help you stay motivated and inspired. It can also lead to more opportunities and valuable connections.

6. **Visualization:** Visualization is a powerful tool for achieving wealth and financial freedom. By visualizing your success and believing that it's possible, you can stay focused and motivated towards your goals. Visualization also helps you stay positive and overcome self-doubt and limiting beliefs.

7. **Belief:** Your beliefs and mindset play a crucial role in your financial success. By developing a positive mindset and believing that wealth is attainable for you, you can overcome any obstacles that come your way. A positive mindset also helps you stay focused on your goals and take consistent action towards them.

8. **Action:** Wealth requires action. By taking deliberate and consistent action towards your goals, you can make progress and achieve success. Action also helps you learn and grow from your experiences, and adjust your strategies as needed.

9. **Gratitude:** Gratitude is an essential component of wealth and financial freedom. By being grateful for what you have and celebrating your successes along the way, you attract more abundance into your life. Gratitude also helps you stay positive and motivated towards your goals, and appreciate the journey towards achieving them.

Overall, the 9 Laws of Wealth provide a framework for achieving wealth and financial freedom. By following these laws, you can develop the skills, mindset, and habits needed to succeed financially. Whether you're just starting out or are already on your journey towards financial freedom, these laws can help you achieve your goals and live the life you want.

CHAPTER ONE

The Law of Clarity

Defining Your Financial Goals And Vision

One of the most important steps in achieving financial success is to have a clear idea of what you want to achieve. Defining your financial goals and vision is essential to creating a roadmap for your financial future. Here are some key points to consider when defining your financial goals and vision:

- **Short-term vs. long-term goals:** It's important to distinguish between short-term and long-term financial goals. Short-term goals are things you want to achieve in the near future, such as paying off credit card debt or saving for a vacation. Long-term goals are things you want to achieve in the distant future, such as retirement or buying a home.

- **Specificity:** The more specific your financial goals, the better. For example, rather than simply saying you want to save more money, set a specific goal such as saving 20% of your income each month.

- **Realistic goals:** While it's important to have ambitious financial goals, it's also important to make sure they are realistic. Setting unattainable goals can be discouraging and lead to a lack of motivation.

- **Prioritization:** When defining your financial goals, it's important to prioritize them. Determine which goals are most important and focus on those first.

Once you have defined your financial goals and vision, the next step is to create a plan to achieve them.

Creating a plan to achieve those goals

Creating a plan to achieve your financial goals is essential to turning them into reality. Here are some key steps to creating a plan:

- **Assess your current situation:** Before creating a plan, it's important to assess your current financial situation. Determine your income, expenses, debts, and assets. This will give you a baseline to work from.

- **Create a budget:** A budget is a key component of any financial plan. It allows you to track your expenses and ensure that you are living within your means. Create a budget that aligns with your financial goals.

- **Set milestones:** Break down your financial goals into smaller, more manageable milestones. This will make them less overwhelming and easier to achieve.

- **Identify potential roadblocks:** Anticipate potential roadblocks that could hinder your progress towards your goals. This could be unexpected expenses, a decrease in income, or a job loss. Having a plan in place to address these roadblocks will help keep you on track.

- **Make adjustments:** Your financial plan should be flexible and adaptable. As your situation changes, adjust your plan accordingly.

With a plan in place, the next step is to focus your attention and intention on achieving your goals.

Understanding The Power Of Focus And Intention

Focus and intention are essential components of achieving financial success. Here's how to harness their power:

- **Eliminate distractions:** Distractions can prevent you from achieving your financial goals. Identify and eliminate any distractions that are hindering your progress. This could be anything from unnecessary spending to social media.

- **Visualize success:** Visualizing success can be a powerful motivator. Picture yourself achieving your financial goals and the positive impact it will have on your life. This will help keep you focused and motivated.

- **Stay positive:** Maintaining a positive mindset is crucial to achieving your financial goals. Focus on your successes and learn from your mistakes. Don't let setbacks discourage you.

- **Take action:** The power of focus and intention lies in taking action. Take consistent, intentional steps towards your financial goals. Even small actions can add up to big results over time.

In conclusion, defining your financial goals and vision, creating a plan to achieve those goals, and harnessing the power of focus and intention are all essential components of achieving financial success.

By taking intentional steps towards your goals, you can create the financial future you desire. Remember that financial success is not achieved overnight and requires patience, persistence, and discipline. With a clear vision, a solid plan, and a focused mindset, you can make your financial dreams a reality. Keep in mind that your financial goals may evolve over time, so it's important to regularly review and adjust your plan as needed.

It's also worth noting that seeking the advice of a financial professional can be beneficial in creating and executing a financial plan. A financial advisor can provide guidance, expertise, and accountability to help you stay on track towards your goals.

In summary, defining your financial goals and vision, creating a plan to achieve those goals, and understanding the power of focus and intention are all crucial components of achieving financial success. By following these steps and staying committed to your plan, you can build a solid financial foundation for yourself and your family.

CHAPTER TWO

The Law of Responsibility

Taking Ownership Of Your Financial Situation

Taking ownership of your financial situation is crucial to achieving financial success. It involves taking responsibility for your financial decisions, being proactive in your financial planning, and developing a long-term financial strategy that aligns with your goals. By taking ownership of your finances, you can gain control over your financial future and make better financial decisions.

Develop a Budget

One way to take ownership of your financial situation is to develop a budget. A budget is a financial plan that outlines your income and expenses, helping you to manage your money more effectively. To create a budget, you will need to track your income and expenses over a period of time, such as a month. This will give you a clear picture of your spending habits and allow you to identify areas where you can cut back. Once you have developed a budget, you should review it regularly and make adjustments as necessary.

Manage Your Debt

Another important step in taking ownership of your financial situation is to manage your debt. This includes paying off high-interest debt, such as credit card balances, as quickly as possible. It also involves avoiding taking on new debt unless it is absolutely necessary. By managing your debt, you can reduce your financial stress and improve your financial situation in the long term.

Invest in Your Future

Taking ownership of your financial situation also involves investing in your future. This includes saving for retirement, building an emergency fund, and investing in education or training that will improve your earning potential. By investing in your future, you can ensure that you have the resources you need to achieve your financial goals and build a secure financial future.

Overcoming Limiting Beliefs And Negative Patterns

Limiting beliefs and negative patterns can hold you back from achieving your goals and living the life you want. These beliefs and patterns can stem from past experiences, cultural conditioning, or personal insecurities. Overcoming them requires self-awareness, commitment, and a willingness to challenge your beliefs and behaviors.

Identify Your Limiting Beliefs

The first step in overcoming limiting beliefs and negative patterns is to identify them. This involves examining your beliefs and behaviors and questioning their validity. Ask yourself if your beliefs are based on fact or if they are just assumptions. Challenge negative self-talk and replace it with positive affirmations. By identifying your limiting beliefs, you can begin to take steps to overcome them.

Change Your Self-Talk

Negative self-talk can reinforce limiting beliefs and negative patterns. To overcome them, you need to change your self-talk. Replace negative thoughts with positive affirmations and focus on your strengths and accomplishments. Surround yourself with positive people who will support and encourage you in your efforts to overcome your limiting beliefs.

Take Action

Overcoming limiting beliefs and negative patterns requires taking action. This involves stepping out of your comfort zone and trying new things. Take small steps towards your goals and celebrate your successes along the way. By taking action, you can build momentum and overcome the self-doubt and fear that can hold you back.

Cultivating A Mindset Of Abundance And Possibility

A mindset of abundance and possibility is a powerful tool for achieving success and happiness in life. It involves focusing on what is possible rather than what is not, and believing that there is enough for everyone to achieve their goals. By cultivating a mindset of abundance and possibility, you can overcome obstacles, achieve your goals, and create a more fulfilling life.

Practice Gratitude

One way to cultivate a mindset of abundance and possibility is to practice gratitude. This involves focusing on what you have rather than what you lack. Make a daily practice of listing things you are grateful for, no matter how small. This can help you shift your focus from scarcity to abundance and create a more positive outlook on life.

Visualize Your Goals

Another important aspect of cultivating a mindset of abundance and possibility is to visualize your goals. Visualization involves imagining yourself achieving your goals in vivid detail. This can help you stay motivated, focused, and committed to your goals. By visualizing your goals, you are programming your subconscious mind to work towards them, and increasing the likelihood of achieving them.

Embrace Change

Embracing change is another key aspect of cultivating a mindset of abundance and possibility. Change can be scary, but it also presents opportunities for growth and learning. Rather than resisting change, embrace it and see it as an opportunity to learn new things and explore new possibilities. By embracing change, you can open yourself up to new opportunities and experiences that can enrich your life.

Take Risks

Taking risks is another important component of cultivating a mindset of abundance and possibility. This involves stepping outside your comfort zone and trying new things, even if they are unfamiliar or challenging. Taking risks can be scary, but it can also lead to great rewards. By taking risks, you can discover new talents, learn new skills, and achieve things you never thought possible.

In conclusion, taking ownership of your financial situation, overcoming limiting beliefs and negative patterns, and cultivating a mindset of abundance and possibility are all important steps towards achieving success and happiness in life. By taking proactive steps to manage your finances, challenging negative beliefs and behaviors, and embracing a positive mindset, you can create a fulfilling and abundant life that is filled with possibilities. Remember, success is not just about achieving your goals, it's about the journey towards them, and the person you become along the way.

CHAPTER THREE

The Law of Investing in Yourself

Prioritizing Personal Growth And Development

Personal growth and development are important aspects of human life. It involves the process of improving oneself in terms of knowledge, skills, and abilities. Personal growth and development can be achieved in several ways, including reading, taking courses, attending workshops and seminars, and seeking mentorship. In today's world, personal growth and development are essential for personal and professional success.

1. Why prioritize personal growth and development?

Personal growth and development help individuals to identify their strengths and weaknesses. This process helps them to understand themselves better and to develop new skills and abilities that will help them achieve their goals. Personal growth and development also enables individuals to improve their relationships with others, as they become better communicators and listeners.

Furthermore, personal growth and development help individuals to increase their confidence, self-esteem, and self-worth. This is because they are continuously improving themselves and achieving their goals, which leads to a sense of accomplishment and satisfaction. Additionally, personal growth and development allow individuals to adapt to changes in their environment, which is critical for success in today's rapidly changing world.

2. How to prioritize personal growth and development?

To prioritize personal growth and development, individuals should set goals and develop a plan to achieve them. These goals can be short-term or long-term, and they should be specific, measurable, achievable, relevant, and time-bound (SMART). Individuals should also identify the resources they need to achieve their goals, including time, money, and support from others.

Moreover, individuals should focus on their strengths and weaknesses and seek ways to improve them. They should also seek feedback from others, including mentors, coaches, and colleagues, to identify areas for improvement. Additionally, individuals should take risks and step out of their comfort zones to learn new skills and gain new experiences.

3. Benefits of prioritizing personal growth and development

There are several benefits of prioritizing personal growth and development. These benefits include:

- Increased self-awareness: Personal growth and development help individuals to understand themselves better, including their strengths, weaknesses, values, and beliefs.
- Improved relationships: Personal growth and development enable individuals to become better communicators and listeners, which leads to

better relationships with others.

- Increased confidence: Personal growth and development help individuals to achieve their goals, which leads to a sense of accomplishment and increased confidence.

- Enhanced creativity: Personal growth and development enable individuals to think outside the box and come up with innovative solutions to problems.

- Improved career prospects: Personal growth and development help individuals to acquire new skills and knowledge that can enhance their career prospects and increase their earning potential.

In conclusion, personal growth and development are essential for personal and professional success. By prioritizing personal growth and development, individuals can identify their strengths and weaknesses, set goals, and develop a plan to achieve them. This process leads to increased self-awareness, improved relationships, increased confidence, enhanced creativity, and improved career prospects.

Developing Skills And Knowledge To Increase Earning Potential

Earning potential refers to the maximum amount an individual can earn in their chosen career. Developing skills and knowledge is an effective way to increase earning potential. In today's world, employers are looking for individuals with diverse skills and knowledge that can contribute to the success of their organization.

1. Why develop skills and knowledge to increase earning

potential?

Developing skills and knowledge is essential for increasing earning potential. This is because employers are willing to pay more for individuals with diverse skills and knowledge that can help them achieve their goals. Furthermore, developing skills and knowledge can lead to career advancement opportunities, which often come with higher salaries and better benefits.

Additionally, developing skills and knowledge can help individuals to stay relevant in their chosen career. This is because industries are constantly changing, and new skills and knowledge are required to stay competitive. By developing new skills and knowledge, individuals can position themselves as experts in their field and increase their value to employers.

2. How to develop skills and knowledge to increase earning potential?

There are several ways to develop skills and knowledge to increase earning potential. Some of these ways include:

- Taking courses: Individuals can take courses to learn new skills and knowledge. This can be done online or in-person, and there are several free and paid courses available.

- Attending workshops and seminars: Workshops and seminars are an effective way to learn new skills and knowledge. These events often provide hands-on training and opportunities to network with other professionals.

- Seeking mentorship: Mentorship is an excellent way to learn from experienced professionals in your field. By seeking mentorship, individuals can gain valuable insights and advice on how to advance their careers.

- Reading: Reading is a great way to learn new skills and knowledge. There are several books and articles available on various topics, and individuals can choose to read based on their interests and goals.

- Participating in online communities: Online communities are a great way to connect with other professionals and learn from their experiences. There are several online communities available, including LinkedIn groups and industry-specific forums.

3. Benefits of developing skills and knowledge to increase earning potential

There are several benefits of developing skills and knowledge to increase earning potential. These benefits include:

- Increased job security: By developing new skills and knowledge, individuals can position themselves as experts in their field. This can increase their job security, as employers are more likely to retain individuals who are valuable to their organization.

- Enhanced career prospects: Developing new skills and knowledge can open up new career opportunities and increase earning potential. This is because individuals who have diverse skills and knowledge are more attractive to employers.

- Increased confidence: By developing new skills and knowledge, individuals can increase their confidence in their abilities. This can lead to better job performance and increased job satisfaction.

- Improved problem-solving skills: Developing new skills and knowledge can help individuals to think critically and come up with innovative solutions to problems. This is a valuable skill in any career.

In conclusion, developing skills and knowledge is essential for increasing earning potential. By taking courses, attending workshops and seminars, seeking mentorship, reading, and participating in online communities, individuals can develop new skills and knowledge that can enhance their career prospects and increase their earning potential.

Investing Time And Resources In Self-Improvement

Investing time and resources in self-improvement is essential for personal and professional growth. Self-improvement involves the process of improving oneself in terms of knowledge, skills, and abilities. By investing time and resources in self-improvement, individuals can achieve their goals, increase their earning potential, and improve their overall quality of life.

1. Why invest time and resources in self-improvement?

Investing time and resources in self-improvement is essential for personal and professional growth. This is because self-improvement enables individuals to identify their strengths and weaknesses, set goals, and develop a plan to achieve them. By investing in self-improvement, individuals can become better versions of themselves and achieve their full potential.

Furthermore, investing in self-improvement can lead to increased confidence, self-esteem, and self-worth. This is because individuals who invest in self-improvement are continuously improving themselves and achieving their goals, which leads to a sense of accomplishment and satisfaction.

2. How to invest time and resources in self-improvement?

There are several ways to invest time and resources in self-improvement. Some of these ways include:

- Setting goals: Individuals should set goals that are specific, measurable, achievable, relevant, and time-bound (SMART). Setting goals helps individuals to identify what they want to achieve and develop a plan to achieve it.

- Seeking feedback: Individuals should seek feedback from others to identify areas where they need to improve. This can be done by asking colleagues, mentors, or friends for constructive feedback.

- Engaging in self-reflection: Individuals should engage in self-reflection to identify areas where they need to improve. This can be done by journaling, meditating, or taking time to reflect on their actions and decisions.

- Taking courses: Individuals can take courses to learn new skills and knowledge. This can be done online or in-person, and there are several free and paid courses available.

- Attending workshops and seminars: Workshops and seminars are an effective way to learn new skills and knowledge. These events often provide hands-on training and opportunities to network with other professionals.

- Seeking mentorship: Mentorship is an excellent way to learn from experienced professionals in your field. By seeking mentorship, individuals can gain valuable insights and advice on how to advance their careers.

- Reading: Reading is a great way to learn new skills and knowledge. There are several books and articles available on various topics, and individuals can choose to read based on their interests and goals.

3. Benefits of investing time and resources in self-improvement

There are several benefits of investing time and resources in self-improvement. These benefits include:

- Personal growth: By investing in self-improvement, individuals can achieve personal growth and become better versions of themselves. This can lead to increased self-esteem, confidence, and overall life satisfaction.

- Professional growth: Investing in self-improvement can lead to increased job performance and career growth. This is because individuals who invest in self-improvement are continuously developing their skills and knowledge, which makes them more valuable to employers.

- Improved relationships: Investing in self-improvement can lead to improved relationships with others. This is because individuals who invest in self-improvement are more self-aware and have better communication skills.

- Increased resilience: By investing in self-improvement, individuals can develop resilience and the ability to overcome challenges. This is because individuals who invest in self-improvement are more likely to have a growth mindset and view challenges as opportunities for growth.

In conclusion, investing time and resources in self-improvement is essential for personal and professional growth. By setting goals, seeking feedback, engaging in self-reflection, taking courses, attending workshops and seminars, seeking mentorship, and reading, individuals can invest in themselves and achieve their full potential.

CHAPTER FOUR

The Law of Saving and Budgeting

Understanding The Importance Of Saving And Budgeting

Saving and budgeting are essential financial skills that everyone should learn. Saving is the process of putting aside money for a specific purpose, while budgeting is the act of planning how you will spend your money. Both are critical in achieving financial stability and reaching your long-term financial goals. In this section, we will discuss the importance of saving and budgeting.

Importance of Saving

Saving is important for several reasons. Firstly, it provides a financial cushion in case of emergencies. Life is unpredictable, and unexpected expenses such as medical bills or car repairs can arise at any time. By having a savings account, you can avoid taking out loans or using credit cards to cover these expenses.

Secondly, saving enables you to achieve your long-term financial goals, such as buying a house, paying for your child's education, or retiring comfortably. By setting aside money regularly, you can accumulate wealth over time and achieve these goals.

Thirdly, saving can help you to reduce financial stress. When you have money saved, you have a sense of security, which can reduce anxiety and stress related to financial matters.

Importance of Budgeting

Budgeting is equally important as saving. It allows you to plan your spending and ensures that you live within your means. With a budget, you can prioritize your expenses, such as paying bills, buying groceries, and paying off debt. It also helps you to identify areas where you can cut back on spending and save more money.

Moreover, budgeting can help you to avoid debt and improve your credit score. By planning your spending, you can avoid overspending and taking on debt, which can negatively impact your credit score.

In summary, saving and budgeting are crucial financial skills that can help you to achieve financial stability, reduce stress, and reach your long-term financial goals.

Creating A Realistic Budget And Sticking To It

Creating a budget can be overwhelming, but it is necessary for achieving financial stability. A budget is a plan for your income and expenses, and it helps you to identify how much money you can spend on different categories such as housing, transportation, food, entertainment, and savings. In this section, we will discuss how to create a realistic budget and stick to it.

Step 1: Determine your income

The first step in creating a budget is to determine your income. This includes your salary, bonuses, and any other sources of income. If you have irregular income, such as freelance work, use an average monthly income for budgeting purposes.

Step 2: Track your expenses

The next step is to track your expenses for a month. This includes all your bills, such as rent/mortgage, utilities, groceries, transportation, entertainment, and any other expenses. You can use a budgeting app or spreadsheet to track your expenses.

Step 3: Categorize your expenses

After tracking your expenses, categorize them into fixed and variable expenses. Fixed expenses are bills that remain constant each month, such as rent/mortgage, while variable expenses fluctuate each month, such as entertainment.

Step 4: Set financial goals

Once you have determined your income and expenses, set financial goals. This could include paying off debt, building an emergency fund, or saving for a down payment on a house.

Step 5: Allocate your income

Allocate your income to each category based on your fixed and variable expenses and financial goals. Make sure to leave some room for unexpected expenses or savings.

Step 6: Monitor your budget

It's important to monitor your budget regularly to ensure that you are staying within your limits. Review your budget each month and make any necessary adjustments to stay on track.

Tips For Sticking To Your Budget

Sticking to a budget can be challenging, but there are several strategies you can use to help you stay on track.

1. Make a commitment to yourself: Creating a budget is one thing, but sticking to it is another. Make a commitment to yourself that you will stick to your budget and make it a priority.

2. Use cash: Using cash for purchases can help you to stay within your budget. Withdraw the amount you have budgeted for each category, and once the cash is gone, you can't spend any more.

3. Avoid impulse purchases: Avoid making impulse purchases by waiting 24 hours before making a purchase. This will give you time to evaluate whether the purchase is necessary or if it will break your budget.

4. Find cheaper alternatives: Look for cheaper alternatives for your expenses. For example, try cooking at home instead of eating out, or find free entertainment options instead of paying for expensive activities.

5. Reward yourself: Set milestones for achieving your financial goals and reward yourself when you reach them. This will help to keep you motivated and on track.

In summary, creating a budget is the first step towards achieving financial stability. By following these steps and strategies, you can create a realistic budget and stick to it, allowing you to reach your financial goals and live within your means.

Strategies For Saving Money And Building Wealth

Saving money and building wealth are essential for achieving financial stability and long-term financial goals. It's important to have a plan in place to save money and build wealth over time. In this section, we will discuss some strategies for saving money and building wealth.

1. Pay yourself first

One of the most important strategies for saving money is to pay yourself first. This means setting aside a portion of your income for savings before paying your bills or expenses. This can be done by setting up automatic transfers to a savings account each month.

2. Cut back on expenses

Cutting back on expenses is another strategy for saving money. Look for areas where you can reduce your spending, such as eating out less, using coupons, or negotiating bills.

3. Start investing

Investing is an essential strategy for building wealth over time. Consider investing in stocks, mutual funds, or other types of investments that align with your financial goals and risk tolerance.

4. Set financial goals

Setting financial goals is crucial for saving money and building wealth. Identify your short-term and long-term financial goals and create a plan to achieve them.

5. Build an emergency fund

Having an emergency fund is important for unexpected expenses and can prevent you from going into debt. Aim to save three to six months' worth of living expenses in an emergency fund.

6. Avoid debt

Avoiding debt is another critical strategy for saving money and building wealth. Try to pay off high-interest debt, such as credit card debt, as quickly as possible, and avoid taking on new debt whenever possible.

7. Live within your means

Finally, living within your means is essential for saving money and building wealth. This means spending less than you earn and avoiding overspending or impulse purchases.

In summary, saving money and building wealth require a long-term plan and commitment. By following these strategies and staying disciplined, you can achieve financial stability and reach your long-term financial goals.

CHAPTER FIVE

The Law of Mindful Spending

Cultivating Awareness And Intention In Your Spending Habits

Cultivating awareness and intention in your spending habits is an essential step towards achieving financial wellness. The first step towards developing good spending habits is becoming aware of your spending patterns. This involves tracking your expenses and identifying areas where you tend to overspend. Once you have identified your spending patterns, you can begin to develop strategies to curb overspending and create healthier spending habits.

One strategy that can help you become more aware of your spending habits is creating a budget. A budget can help you set limits on your spending and allocate your resources towards achieving your financial goals. When creating a budget, it is important to prioritize your spending, focusing on the expenses that are essential for your wellbeing and financial stability.

Another strategy for cultivating awareness and intention in your spending habits is practicing mindfulness. Mindfulness involves paying attention to the present moment without judgment. By being mindful of your spending, you can become more aware of the emotions and impulses that drive your spending habits. This awareness can help you identify triggers that lead to impulse purchases and unnecessary spending.

Avoiding Impulse Purchases And Unnecessary Expenses

One of the biggest obstacles to cultivating awareness and intention in your spending habits is impulse purchases and unnecessary expenses. Impulse purchases are unplanned and often driven by emotions, such as boredom or stress. Unnecessary expenses, on the other hand, are expenses that are not essential for your wellbeing or financial stability.

To avoid impulse purchases and unnecessary expenses, it is important to practice self-control and discipline. One way to do this is by creating a waiting period before making a purchase. This waiting period can help you evaluate whether the purchase is necessary and aligns with your financial goals.

Another strategy for avoiding impulse purchases and unnecessary expenses is creating a shopping list. A shopping list can help you stay focused on the items that you need and avoid purchasing items that are not essential. Additionally, it can be helpful to avoid shopping when you are feeling emotional or stressed, as these emotions can lead to impulse purchases.

Making Conscious Choices That Align With Your Financial Goals

Making conscious choices that align with your financial goals is essential for achieving financial wellness. When making financial decisions, it is important to consider the long-term impact of your choices on your financial wellbeing. This involves setting clear financial goals and developing a plan to achieve them.

One way to make conscious choices that align with your financial goals is by prioritizing your spending. Prioritizing your spending involves focusing on the expenses that are essential for your wellbeing and financial stability. This may involve cutting back on unnecessary expenses, such as dining out or entertainment, to allocate more resources towards achieving your financial goals.

Another strategy for making conscious choices that align with your financial goals is investing in your future. Investing in your future involves allocating resources towards long-term financial goals, such as retirement or education. This may involve saving a portion of your income or investing in stocks or real estate.

Finally, it is important to practice patience and discipline when making financial decisions. This involves avoiding impulsive decisions and taking the time to evaluate the long-term impact of your choices on your financial wellbeing. By cultivating awareness and intention in your spending habits, avoiding impulse purchases and unnecessary expenses, and making conscious choices that align with your financial goals, you can achieve financial wellness and long-term financial stability.

CHAPTER SIX

The Law of Investing in Assets

Understanding The Different Types Of Assets

Assets are resources that an individual or organization owns or controls with the expectation that they will generate future value. In investing, assets are essential components of a diversified portfolio, and understanding the different types of assets is critical to making informed investment decisions.

Cash and Cash Equivalents: Cash and cash equivalents are highly liquid assets that include bank deposits, money market funds, and short-term government securities. Cash and cash equivalents are low-risk, low-return assets that provide stability to an investment portfolio.

Fixed Income Securities: Fixed income securities, also known as bonds, are debt instruments issued by corporations, governments, or other organizations to raise capital. Bonds typically pay a fixed rate of interest to investors, making them a popular choice for income-oriented investors.

Equities: Equities, also known as stocks or shares, represent ownership in a company. When an individual invests in equities, they become a shareholder in the company, giving them the right to vote on company decisions and receive a share of profits in the form of dividends.

Real Estate: Real estate refers to physical property such as land, buildings, and houses. Real estate can provide both rental income and capital appreciation, making it a popular choice for long-term investors.

Commodities: Commodities are raw materials such as gold, silver, oil, and agricultural products that are traded on commodity exchanges. Commodities can provide diversification to an investment portfolio and are often used as a hedge against inflation.

Alternative Investments: Alternative investments include assets that do not fit into the traditional categories of stocks, bonds, and cash. These can include hedge funds, private equity, venture capital, and real assets such as art, wine, and collectibles.

Developing A Strategy For Investing In Assets

Developing a strategy for investing in assets involves determining your investment goals, risk tolerance, and time horizon. It also involves creating a diversified portfolio that includes a mix of asset classes and individual investments. Here are some steps to follow when developing an investment strategy:

1. Determine Your Investment Goals: Before investing, you need to define your investment goals. Are you looking to generate income, grow your wealth, or achieve a specific financial objective such as buying a house or funding your retirement?

2. Assess Your Risk Tolerance: Every investor has a different tolerance for risk. Some are comfortable with high-risk investments that offer the potential for high returns, while others prefer low-risk investments that offer more stability. Understanding your risk tolerance is important when selecting investments.

3. Determine Your Time Horizon: Your time horizon refers to the length of time you plan to hold your investments. Investors with a longer time horizon can typically afford to take more risk, as they have more time to recover from market downturns.

4. Create a Diversified Portfolio: Diversification involves spreading your investments across a variety of asset classes and individual investments. This can help reduce your overall risk and improve your chances of achieving your investment goals.

5. Monitor and Rebalance Your Portfolio: As market conditions change, it's important to monitor and rebalance your portfolio to ensure it remains aligned with your investment goals and risk tolerance.

Maximizing The Return On Your Investments

Maximizing the return on your investments involves making smart investment decisions and managing your investments effectively. Here are some tips for maximizing your investment returns:

1. Start Early: The earlier you start investing, the more time your investments have to grow. Even small contributions to your investment portfolio can add up over time.

2. Invest Regularly: Investing regularly, such as through a monthly contribution to your investment portfolio, can help smooth out market volatility and build wealth over time.

3. Minimize Fees: Fees can eat into your investment returns, so it's important to choose investments with low fees and expenses. Consider using low-cost index funds or ETFs to minimize fees and maximize returns.

4. Stay Invested for the Long-Term: Trying to time the market or make short-term trades can be risky and result in lower returns. Instead, focus on a long-term investment strategy and stick to it, even during market downturns.

5. Reinvest Dividends and Capital Gains: Reinvesting dividends and capital gains can help your investments grow over time. This can be done automatically through a dividend reinvestment plan (DRIP) or by manually reinvesting your earnings.

6. Keep an Eye on Taxes: Taxes can impact your investment returns, so it's important to consider the tax implications of your investments. Consider using tax-advantaged accounts such as IRAs or 401(k)s to minimize taxes on your investments.

7. Stay Educated: The investment landscape is constantly changing, so it's important to stay informed and educated about new investment opportunities and market trends. Consider reading financial news, attending investment seminars, or working with a financial advisor to stay up-to-date on the latest investment strategies.

In conclusion, understanding the different types of assets, developing a strategy for investing in assets, and maximizing the return on your investments are all important components of successful investing. By diversifying your portfolio, minimizing fees, and staying invested for the long-term, you can maximize your investment returns and achieve your financial goals.

CHAPTER SEVEN

The Law of Passive Income

Creating Passive Income Streams To Supplement Your Earnings

Passive income streams have become a popular way for people to supplement their earnings and achieve financial freedom. This form of income can be generated from various sources, including real estate, investing, online businesses, and more. In this article, we will explore what passive income is and how you can create passive income streams to supplement your earnings.

What is Passive Income?

Passive income is money that you earn without actively working for it. It is a form of income that requires little to no effort to maintain once the initial work has been completed. Unlike active income, where you exchange your time and effort for money, passive income streams allow you to earn money even when you're not working.

Understanding the Different Types of Passive Income

There are various types of passive income streams that you can create. Some of the most common ones include:

Real Estate - This involves purchasing a property and

renting it out to tenants. You can earn a steady stream of passive income from the rental payments without having to do much work.

Investing - This includes investing in stocks, bonds, mutual funds, and other investment vehicles. The idea is to earn a return on your investment without actively managing it.

Online Businesses - You can create an online business that generates passive income, such as creating an e-commerce store, a blog, or an affiliate marketing website.

Digital Products - This includes creating and selling digital products such as e-books, courses, and software. Once you've created these products, you can sell them repeatedly without having to create new ones.

Strategies For Building Passive Income Over Time

Creating passive income streams takes time and effort, but the rewards can be significant. Here are some strategies that you can use to build passive income over time:

1. Set Realistic Goals - It's important to set realistic goals when it comes to building passive income streams. Determine how much you want to earn and by when. This will help you stay focused and motivated.

2. Invest in Yourself - To create passive income streams, you need to invest in yourself. This includes learning new skills, taking courses, and reading books on topics related to passive income.

3. Start Small - You don't need to start with a large investment or a complex business idea. Start small and build your way up. For example, you can start by investing in a single stock or creating a simple e-commerce store.

4. Diversify Your Income Streams - To reduce your risk and increase your chances of success, it's important to diversify your income streams. Don't rely on a single source of passive income. Instead, create multiple streams of income from different sources.

5. Be Patient - Building passive income streams takes time. Don't expect to see results overnight. Stay patient and consistent with your efforts, and you'll eventually see the results.

6. Leverage Technology - There are many tools and platforms available that can help you create and manage passive income streams. Take advantage of these tools to streamline your processes and make your life easier.

CHAPTER EIGHT

The Law of Giving Back

Cultivating A Mindset Of Generosity And Abundance

Cultivating a mindset of generosity and abundance is a powerful way to live your life. This mindset is about adopting a positive outlook towards life, believing in the abundance of the universe and being willing to give and receive. With this mindset, you can tap into the power of the law of attraction and create a life of abundance and prosperity.

One way to cultivate this mindset is by practicing gratitude. When you focus on what you have instead of what you lack, you shift your attention to the positive aspects of your life. This shift in perspective can help you feel more content, fulfilled, and happy.

Another way to cultivate a mindset of generosity is by being willing to give to others. This can be in the form of time, money, or other resources. When you give to others, you create a sense of abundance and you feel good about yourself. Giving also creates a ripple effect, inspiring others to give back as well.

It's important to note that cultivating a mindset of

generosity and abundance is not about giving away everything you have. It's about finding a balance between giving and receiving, and recognizing that you have enough to share with others.

Understanding The Power Of Giving Back To Others

Giving back to others is a powerful way to make a positive impact on the world. It can also have a significant impact on your own life. When you give back, you create a sense of purpose and meaning, and you can experience a greater sense of fulfillment and satisfaction.

One way to give back is by volunteering your time. There are countless organizations and causes that need volunteers, and your skills and expertise can make a big difference. Volunteering can also provide you with new experiences and skills, and can help you connect with others in your community.

Another way to give back is by making a financial contribution. Charitable donations can support organizations and causes that are important to you, and can help make a difference in the lives of others. When you make a donation, you can also benefit from tax deductions and other financial incentives.

It's important to remember that giving back is not just about the impact you can make on others. It's also about the impact it can have on you. Giving back can help you develop a sense of empathy and compassion, and can help you appreciate the blessings in your own life.

Incorporating Charitable Giving Into Your Financial Plan

Incorporating charitable giving into your financial plan can be a powerful way to align your values with your financial goals. There are several ways to do this.

One way is by setting aside a portion of your income for charitable donations. This can be a fixed amount or a percentage of your income. By incorporating charitable giving into your budget, you can ensure that you are contributing to causes that are important to you, while also maintaining your financial goals.

Another way to incorporate charitable giving into your financial plan is by setting up a donor-advised fund. This is a charitable giving account that allows you to make donations to charitable organizations over time. Donor-advised funds can provide you with tax benefits, and can help you plan your giving over the long-term.

You can also consider incorporating charitable giving into your estate planning. By leaving a portion of your assets to charitable organizations in your will, you can create a lasting impact on causes that are important to you, while also benefiting from tax deductions.

Regardless of how you choose to incorporate charitable giving into your financial plan, it's important to do so in a way that aligns with your values and goals. By doing so, you can create a sense of purpose and fulfillment, while also making a positive impact on the world.

CHAPTER NINE

The Law of Persistence

Overcoming Obstacles And Setbacks

Life is full of obstacles and setbacks that can derail us from our goals and aspirations. These challenges can come in different forms, such as financial difficulties, health problems, career setbacks, or personal struggles. However, how we respond to these obstacles and setbacks is what makes the difference between success and failure.

One of the first steps in overcoming obstacles and setbacks is to acknowledge their existence and accept them as part of the journey towards success. It is natural to feel discouraged, frustrated, or overwhelmed when facing challenges, but these emotions should not paralyze us. Instead, we should view obstacles and setbacks as opportunities to learn, grow, and become more resilient.

To overcome obstacles and setbacks, it is essential to have a growth mindset. A growth mindset is the belief that our abilities, skills, and intelligence can be developed through dedication, effort, and persistence. In contrast, a fixed mindset is the belief that our abilities and intelligence are fixed and cannot be changed.

With a growth mindset, we can approach obstacles and

setbacks as opportunities for growth and learning. Instead of giving up, we can try new approaches, seek feedback, learn from our mistakes, and persist in our efforts. This mindset shift can help us overcome self-doubt, fear of failure, and negative self-talk that can hinder our progress.

Another key factor in overcoming obstacles and setbacks is to have a support system. No one can succeed alone, and having people who believe in us, encourage us, and provide practical help can make a significant difference. This support system can come from family, friends, mentors, coaches, or colleagues who share our goals and values.

Finally, overcoming obstacles and setbacks requires perseverance and resilience. Perseverance is the ability to keep going despite challenges, setbacks, or failures. Resilience is the ability to bounce back from adversity, learn from it, and grow stronger. These qualities can be developed through practice, discipline, and commitment to our goals.

In conclusion, overcoming obstacles and setbacks is not easy, but it is possible. By having a growth mindset, a support system, and perseverance and resilience, we can overcome challenges, learn from them, and achieve our goals.

Staying Motivated And Focused On Your Goals

Motivation and focus are critical ingredients for achieving our goals and aspirations. Motivation is the driving force that propels us towards our goals, while focus is the ability to stay on track and avoid distractions or detours.

However, staying motivated and focused can be challenging, especially when facing competing demands, distractions, or setbacks. Here are some strategies that can help:

1. Clarify your why: Having a clear understanding of why your goals matter to you can provide a sense of purpose and motivation. When you know your why, you are more likely to stay committed to your goals, even when facing challenges or setbacks.

2. Set SMART goals: SMART goals are Specific, Measurable, Achievable, Relevant, and Time-bound. By setting SMART goals, you can break down your big goals into smaller, manageable steps, track your progress, and stay motivated by seeing your achievements.

3. Create a plan: A plan can provide a roadmap for achieving your goals, identify potential obstacles, and outline the steps you need to take. When you have a plan, you are more likely to stay focused and avoid distractions or procrastination.

4. Develop a routine: A routine can help you establish good habits, reduce decision fatigue, and create a sense of structure and consistency. When you have a routine, you are more likely to stay focused and motivated, even when facing unexpected events or disruptions.

5. Find inspiration and accountability: Inspiration can come from different sources, such as books, podcasts, mentors, or role models. When you find inspiration, you can renew your motivation and stay focused on your goals. Accountability can come from having someone who checks in with you, provides feedback, or supports your progress. When you have accountability, you are more likely to stay committed and follow through on your plans.

6. Practice self-care: Self-care is essential for maintaining your motivation and focus. When you take care of your physical, emotional, and mental health, you are more likely to have the energy, resilience, and clarity needed to pursue your goals. Self-care can include exercise, sleep, healthy eating, relaxation, and self-reflection.

In conclusion, staying motivated and focused on your goals requires a combination of strategies and habits that can help you overcome obstacles, stay committed, and achieve your aspirations.

The Importance Of Perseverance In Building Wealth

Perseverance is a vital quality for building wealth and financial success. Perseverance is the ability to keep going despite challenges, setbacks, or failures. It is the determination to pursue your goals, even when the road is tough, and the obstacles seem insurmountable.

In building wealth, perseverance is essential because it takes time, effort, and discipline to achieve financial stability and independence. Wealth is not built overnight, but through consistent and deliberate actions that accumulate over time.

To persevere in building wealth, it is essential to have a long-term perspective. A long-term perspective means focusing on the big picture and the ultimate goal, rather than short-term gains or losses. It means understanding that wealth-building is a marathon, not a sprint, and that setbacks and fluctuations are part of the journey.

Another key factor in building wealth through perseverance is to develop good financial habits. Good financial habits can include budgeting, saving, investing, and managing debt. These habits require discipline, consistency, and a willingness to delay gratification in the short term for long-term gains.

To build wealth through perseverance, it is also essential to learn from mistakes and failures. Financial mistakes and failures are inevitable, but they can also be valuable lessons that help us improve our strategies, avoid future pitfalls, and grow our knowledge and skills. By learning from mistakes and failures, we can become more resilient and adaptable, and increase our chances of success.

Finally, building wealth through perseverance requires a willingness to take calculated risks. Calculated risks are risks that are based on sound research, analysis, and planning, rather than impulsive or reckless decisions. Taking calculated risks can involve investing in stocks, real estate, or starting a business, among others. These risks can offer potential rewards, but they also involve uncertainty, volatility, and the possibility of losses.

CONCLUSION:

Summary Of The 9 Laws Of Wealth

The 9 Laws of Wealth are principles that can help individuals build wealth and achieve financial success. They were developed by author and financial expert, Dr. Daniel Crosby. Let's take a look at each of these laws:

1. The Law of Purpose - This law suggests that individuals need to have a clear purpose or goal in order to achieve financial success. It's important to know what you want and why you want it.

2. The Law of Planning - This law emphasizes the importance of creating a plan and sticking to it. Without a plan, it's easy to get sidetracked and lose sight of your goals.

3. The Law of Diligence - This law stresses the importance of hard work and persistence. Building wealth requires consistent effort over time.

4. The Law of Patience - This law reminds us that building wealth takes time. It's important to be patient and stay focused on the long-term.

5. The Law of Integrity - This law emphasizes the importance of honesty and integrity in all

financial dealings. Without trust, it's difficult to build and maintain wealth.

6. The Law of Gratitude - This law encourages individuals to cultivate a sense of gratitude for what they have. Gratitude helps individuals stay focused on what's important and avoid the trap of constantly wanting more.

7. The Law of Giving - This law suggests that giving back is an important part of building wealth. Helping others can bring a sense of purpose and fulfillment that money alone can't provide.

8. The Law of Association - This law emphasizes the importance of surrounding yourself with positive influences. Building relationships with successful and like-minded individuals can help you stay motivated and focused.

9. The Law of Education - This law stresses the importance of continuing education and personal growth. Learning new skills and staying up-to-date on industry trends can help individuals stay ahead of the curve and achieve financial success.

Action steps for implementing these laws in your life

While the 9 Laws of Wealth may sound simple, putting them into practice can be challenging. Here are some action steps you can take to implement these laws in your life:

1. Define your purpose - Take some time to think about what you want to achieve and why. Write down your goals and create a plan for achieving them.

2. Create a financial plan - Identify your income

sources and expenses, and create a budget that aligns with your goals. Make sure to include saving and investing as part of your plan.

3. Cultivate a strong work ethic - Set clear goals for yourself and work hard to achieve them. Stay focused and consistent, even when things get challenging.

4. Practice patience - Recognize that building wealth takes time and stay focused on the long-term. Don't get discouraged by short-term setbacks or fluctuations in the market.

5. Emphasize honesty and integrity in all your financial dealings - Be transparent and upfront in your communications with others. Build trust by always doing what you say you'll do.

6. Cultivate gratitude - Take time to appreciate the things you have and the progress you've made. This can help you stay motivated and focused on your goals.

7. Give back to others - Find ways to help others and give back to your community. This can provide a sense of purpose and fulfillment beyond financial success.

8. Surround yourself with positive influences - Seek out relationships with people who are supportive and motivating. Stay away from negative influences that can bring you down.

9. Continuously educate yourself - Stay up-to-date on industry trends and best practices. Invest in your personal growth and development by taking courses or attending conferences.

The potential for financial freedom and abundance by following these laws

Following the 9 Laws of Wealth can help individuals achieve financial freedom and abundance.

By defining your purpose and creating a financial plan, you can set yourself up for long-term success. Cultivating a strong work ethic, practicing patience, and emphasizing honesty and integrity can help you stay on track and build trust with others. Gratitude, giving back, surrounding yourself with positive influences, and continuously educating yourself can help you maintain a sense of purpose and fulfillment beyond financial success.

Implementing these laws in your life can lead to financial freedom and abundance in a number of ways. For example, by creating a budget and saving consistently, you can build up an emergency fund and save for long-term goals like retirement. By investing in your personal growth and development, you can increase your earning potential and build a successful career. By surrounding yourself with positive influences, you can build a network of supportive contacts that can open up new opportunities and help you achieve your goals.

In addition to these tangible benefits, following the 9 Laws of Wealth can also lead to a sense of personal fulfillment and happiness. By defining your purpose and focusing on what's truly important, you can avoid the trap of constantly wanting more and instead appreciate the things you have. Giving back to others and cultivating a sense of gratitude can bring a sense of joy and fulfillment that money alone can't provide.

Overall, the potential for financial freedom and abundance

by following the 9 Laws of Wealth is significant. By implementing these laws in your life and staying focused on your long-term goals, you can build a successful and fulfilling financial future.

www.ingramcontent.com/pod-product-compliance
Lightning Source LLC
Chambersburg PA
CBHW070757220526
45467CB00014B/691